MW01280114

Your Incredible
Mind

HOW TO REPROGRAM YOUR SUBCONSCIOUS
MIND TO LIVE YOUR BEST LIFE AT ANY AGE

ZARINAH EL-AMIN MAJIED

BOOK POWER PUBLISHING
Detroit, MI

Your Incredible Mind: How to reprogram your subconscious mind to live your best life at any age

Copyright © 2019 by Zarinah El-Amin Majied

Published by Book Power Publishing, A division of Niyah Press
www.bookpowerpublishing.com

Book Power books may be purchased for educational, business, or sales promotional use.

For information, please write the author directly: beaboutu@gmail.com

ISBN: 978-1-945873-28-7

Personal Development / Spirituality / Quality of Life

I dedicate this book to my mother (may her grave be spacious and light), my children who were the wind beneath my wings, and my loving and supportive husband.

I acknowledge all the strong women who came before me in my family, women who endured abuse and pain. I humbly bow to the greatness in them that wasn't realized.

Contents

Key Terms

ALLAH means G-D in Arabic, the hyphen is used to have respect so that the word is not reversed to dog

Alhamdulillah: All Praises Due to G-D

PBUH: Peace Be Upon Him

BISMILLAH
(With The Name of G-D)

Introduction

> *"The LORD chose Adam (for HIS Grace):*
> *HE turned to him, and gave him guidance*
>
> The Holy Quran, 20:122

HAVE YOU EVER thought or said, "If I had known at 20 or 30 years old what I know now, I would have done things a lot differently?" Well, a different way might have been all fine and good if G-D had wanted it that way. However, I realize that some of my most significant learning came from the experiences and knowledge I gained along the way, most of which came after age 20 and even after 40. So, even if I could go back, I would probably make the same choices considering the limited knowledge I possessed.

The one thing I wish I had understood better at a young age was the power of my mind. What I've come to learn is that our brain was designed differently than any other created mammal. With our minds, we can literally change how we experience this life. That is why I wanted to write *Your Incredible Mind* to share my journey and my transformation using my mind.

Are you at a place where you're feeling like you'd like to do something else with your life but you're not really sure what? Or you know what you want to do but don't know how to make it happen? Well learning about your incredible mind is the answer to these dilemmas.

The breakthroughs I've witnessed from women going from not knowing to knowing has been phenomenal. One experience was with a woman that felt she was stuck in the routine of being a housewife. She felt her dreams and aspirations were unattainable. Through working on the power of the subconscious mind and the learning that she had control of her destiny, her life took on a new meaning. Once she changed her mindset and started moving towards her dreams,her family rallied behind her and supported her in her renewed way of being.

Being a part of a woman's journey to renewed freedom is the most rewarding benefit as a Health Coach. Helping women to realize better health, renewed energy, or supporting them through their transformation is worth its weight in gold. Working together, crying together, and celebrating the wins is medicine for the soul, and it can happen through the workings of our incredible mind

So, if you're at a stage in your life that you're looking to create the life you want, then you've picked up the right book. I will share with you the techniques I've used to obtain the things I've desired in my life. These techniques will be tools you can begin to use immediately. I will share more about how our minds work and how you can gain control over your destiny. G-D has given us all what we need to have a fruitful and rewarding life; we just have to learn how to access it.

"Ask, and it will be given to you; seek, and you will find; knock, and it will be opened to you. For everyone who asks receives, and he who seeks finds, and to him who knocks it will be opened."

—*Book of Matthew 7:7–8*

CHAPTER 1
The Subconscious Mind

"And HE taught Adam the names of all things"

The Holy Quran, 2:31

THE GEM WITHIN

WHAT IS THE subconscious mind? Is this a question you've ever given any real thought to?

Well as I began to ponder over it, it became clear that it wasn't an organ like our brain or other identifiable body parts. So then my question was, is the subconscious mind the soul, which is spoke about in religious and spiritual settings. In the Holy Quran, 17:85:

> *"And they ask you concerning the soul. Say: "The soul is one of the things, of which the knowledge is only with my Lord. And of knowledge, you (mankind) have been given only a little."*

This verse doesn't say whether the mind and soul are the same, so I was left to theorize what it is as did Rev. William T. Walsh, a historian, educator, and author, who quoted in the book *The Secret of the Ages,* by Robert Collier:

The subconscious part in us is called the subjective mind, because it does not decide and command. It is a subject rather than a ruler. Its nature is to do what it is told or what really in your heart of hearts you desire.[1]

What I have found is that this statement represents the consensus of the other self-help advocates who have written or spoken about the power of the subconscious mind. I've concluded that the subconscious mind is a precious gem that was given to us by G-D to assist us in creating a life of our own choosing once we understand and implement the power of it in our lives.

---

1   Robert Collier, *The Secret of the Ages* (New York: P. F. Collier & Son Co. Inc, 1926), Page 45

When we think about all the advances that human beings have made since our beginning, we have to wonder what guided them along. All we had to work with were plants, animals, insects, and nature. We had no form of communication with others who were not in hollering distance of us, and our form of transportation was walking, or an animal we had to tame. And yet today, we can communicate with people on the other side of the world using a device that isn't connected visibly to anything, and we can fly across the world in a few hours.

I thank G-D everyday for guiding me to the knowledge of how the subconscious mind works and how its incredible power is available to every human being. This knowledge has opened up so many possibilities in a life I thought was headed nowhere. Prior to my awakening, my outlook on life was very negative, and my thoughts were self-defeating and unmotivating.

As G-D says in the verse quoted at the beginning of this chapter, Adam, who represents all human beings, was taught the name of all things, and given dominion over other created things. What a blessing to know that we were given special abilities that weren't afforded to any other created being. We were given a force inside of us, which man has named the subconscious mind, that can literally take us to the moon or send us into the depths of despair.

G-D says in The Holy Quran, 95:4–6:

---

4. *"We have indeed created man in the best of moulds"*
5. *"Then do We abase him (to be) the lowest of the low"*
6. *"Except such as believe and do righteous deeds; for they shall have a reward unfailing"*

Gaining an understanding of my given ability to orchestrate my life using my mind was a game changer for me. The fact that I'm writing this book is a testament to the power of the subconscious mind. Thirty plus years ago, I was told I'd be an author, but I told myself that would never happen. It wasn't until I started to use the techniques and exercises I will share with you in this book that the prophecy became a reality.

FERTILE SOIL

"As a man thinketh in his heart, so is he."

— *Holy Bible,* Book of Proverbs, 23:7

Have you ever seen a garden so beautiful that you had to stop and savor the various colors, smells, and arrangement? Did you stop to reflect that this work of art came from someone's mind? Maybe not, because usually we just admire the beauty of it, and not think of the mind that the vision came from. But when you think about it, everything we see in creation that is man-made came from someone's mind. It was a thought or a vision that turned into reality. In the case of the garden, the gardener had a vision or a thought of how he or she wanted the garden to look. Then, the gardener had to get the right seeds or plants, prepare the soil, plant, and learn how to properly take care of the garden before it could become a master-piece for others to enjoy.

Our minds are like the garden. If we have a thought (seed), it becomes planted in our subconscious mind (fertile soil), and what that seed grows into depends on whether it was a positive or negative thought. Our subconscious mind will only give us back want we plant in it. If the seed (thought) was a self-defeating thought, it will produce a self-defeating attitude. Whereas if the seed (thought) is of self-love and love of others, it will produce an attitude of love.

We come into this world with fertile soil that is prepared for planting. Our caregivers are the gardeners and the thoughts and messages (seeds) they plant can produce beautiful flowers or destructive weeds. So if the thoughts and messages are of a constructive nature, filled with care, and love the end result can be a beautiful garden. However, if the thoughts and messages are tainted with criticism, belittlement, and a lack of love, then the garden can be filled with destructive weeds. The latter is my story.

I am the youngest of my mother's three children—the only one she raised. My mother relocated to California leaving my sister and brother with relatives in Mobile, Alabama. I believe her goal was to create for herself a new life in California. So her getting pregnant with me a year later was clearly not apart of the plan. I thank G-D that, due to her Christian upbringing, aborting me wasn't an option.

After our mother passed, I learned from my sister that our mother had wanted to take me to the relatives in Alabama, but that didn't work.

I know my mother loved me in her dysfunctional way. Her answer to giving her children the best care was to allow someone else to raise them. As I grew up, criticism was the dominant thought and messages (seeds) planted in my subconscious mind (fertile soil). This resulted in feelings of unworthiness, unloved and not being good enough. What I learned after my mother's death is that these negative messages were planted in her fertile soil even before birth. My grandmother was a victim of physical abuse while she was pregnant with my mother, and the abuse continued until my mother left around the age of 20.

My sister was told by an aunt that married into the family, that our mother was treated like a servant as a child and denied the opportunity to go beyond elementary school. She was also violated by a family member and became pregnant, which produced my sister.

The anger and pain she carried with her all her life was demonstrated in her parenting. So, as you can probably guess, my garden was infested with a lot of weeds. She planted a bushel of negative messages (seeds) in my fertile soil (subconscious mind) not realizing the damage it was doing. I had low self-esteem, didn't think I was very smart, lacked confidence, and felt that I did not belong. But as I said earlier, that all changed when I learned about the power of the subconscious mind and how it could be our navigator through this complex world.

NAVIGATOR

The word *navigator* means, *"A person that directs the route or course of a ship, aircraft, or other form of transportation."* Our conscious mind is our navigator. It directs the course of our life through the thoughts and messages we plant in our subconscious mind. .

In 1957, Earl Nightingale, a motivational speaker, produced a spoken word record called *The Strangest Secret*. One of the stories was about a man he saw operating this huge tractor while he was traveling along a highway. What came to his mind was how small the man looked operating this huge tractor. He compared that visual to how our conscious and subconscious mind works. He thought of the tractor as representing the subconscious mind, and the man being the conscious. If the man doesn't guide the direction of the tractor, it could end up in a ditch. Which is what can happen when we are not monitoring the thoughts and messages we plant in our subconscious mind, we could end up in unfavorable situations or circumstance. Our conscious mind is like the captain of a ship navigating the course of our destiny. Where we end up is all in how we set our sails.

A poem by Ella Wheeler Wilcox, an American author and poet, said it very poetically in the book, *The Secret of the Ages*:

> One ship drives east, and another drives west,
> With the self-same winds that blow.
> 'Tis the set of the sails, and not the gales
> Which tells us the way they go.
> Like the waves of the sea are the ways of fate
> As we voyage along thru life
> 'Tis the set of the soul which decides its goal
> And not the calm or the strife.[2]

Jim Rohn, one of my favorite motivational speakers who was also an author and entrepreneur said, "It is the setting of the sails, not the direction of the wind that determines

---

2 Collier, *Secret of the Ages*, Page 263.

which way we will go."[3] Our destination in this journey called life is up to us. We have to decide where we want to go; then, we have to impress that on our subconscious mind, and it will take us there.

OUR HUMBLE SERVANT

The human being was given special abilities that weren't afforded to any other created being. We were given the ability to change our destiny. Everything else in creation is destined to be whatever it was created to be. Trees, cats, dogs, insects, the galaxies, etc. can only be what it was created to be. There is a line from a play called, *The Secret of Freedom,* written by Pulitzer Prize-winner Archibald MacLeish that goes straight to the point:

"The only thing about a man that is a man is his mind. Everything else you can find in a pig or a horse."[4]

---

3 YouTube video submitted by Inner Perceptions
4 Internet Archive Books-Three Short Stories-Archive.org

The irony is that G-D has been giving us some instructions along the way in scripture like in The Holy Bible, Mark 11:24 says:

"Whatsoever thing ye desire when ye pray, pray as if ye had already received and ye shall have."

The Holy Quran, 32:9:

9. "But HE fashioned him in due proportion, and breathed into him something of HIS spirit. And HE gave you (the faculties of) hearing and sight and feeling (and understanding): little thanks do ye give"

Our humble servant is waiting to serve us and to help us achieve our heart's desire, but it needs our conscious participation. Stand guard over what messages and thoughts go into your subconscious mind. Ensure that it will produce for you the life you want.

Busy your mind with the concepts of harmony, health, peace, and goodwill, and wonders will happen in your life.[5]

—Joseph Murphy

5 Joseph Murphy, *The Power of the Subconscious Mind* (Digireads.com, Publishing).

Your Incredible Mind
Action

On a 5 x 7 card, write on one side something you want that is abstract (e.g., confidence, more focused, etc.) or tangible (e.g., job, lose weight, money).

On the other side, write the verse from the Book of Matthew: (1) seek and you shall find, (2) ask and it will be given to you, and (3) knock and it will be open to you.

Read this card every day for the next 30 days with feeling, having faith and belief. Witness and record the results.

CHAPTER 2
Programming

OLD TAPES

*O*UR SUBCONSCIOUS MIND is a built-in tape recorder. From the day we're born, our mind records everything we see, hear, smell, or touch. Our internal tape recorder is constantly storing all the messages it receives from the people and things in our environment. Depending on how aware our caregivers are, the messages may be positive or negative.

When you watch children, you can get a glimpse of what messages are being planted in their subconscious minds by their actions and behavior. I have grandchildren whose parents pray in their presence often, and recite certain words, which the grandchildren will imitate while playing. They will also make statements and say words that you know they've heard from an adult.

Wherever we are in life it is a reflection of our thought patterns. If we are not consciously questioning our actions, or monitoring our thoughts we will be doing or saying things that originated from someone else's reality.

For example, I heard a story about a woman who always cut off the end of her roast before she cooked it. One day, someone asked her why she did that, and she replied that's what she saw her mother and grandmother do. When they inquired from others why the grandmother cut off the end of her roast, they were told that she did so because the pan she used to cook the roast was too small, so she had to cut off the end to make it fit!

In his book *What to Say When You Talk to Yourself*, Shad Helmstetter, PhD, states:

By the time most of us reach adulthood, we are so conditioned to think in a certain way that our pattern remains that way. How we look at life, what we believe about ourselves, how we view anything, and what we do about it, gets filtered through our preconceptions.[6]

Fortunately, if the thoughts and ideas that have been planted in our subconscious mind are counterproductive to what we want in our life, we can erase the negative thought pattern and replace it with new and more productive messages—much like you can do with a tape recorder. However, with a tape recorder, you can erase and record something new in one sitting, and it's done. With our subconscious mind, the process of replacing old recordings takes a little longer. I use to hear that it takes 21 to 30 days to change a habit, however today they're saying at least 66 days. In my experience it definitely has taken longer than 21-30 days to rewire the brain to incorporate a new habit, and this is if you're consistent.

Mahatma Gandhi said:

---

6 Shad Helmstetter, *What to Say When You Talk to Yourself* (New York: Pocket Books, 1982), Page 61.

Man often becomes what he believes himself to be. If I keep on saying to myself that I cannot do a certain thing, it is possible that I may end by really becoming incapable of doing it. On the contrary, if I have the belief that I can do it, I shall surely acquire the capacity to do it even if I may not have it at the beginning.[7]

Monitor Your Thoughts and Thinking

It has been estimated that between 50,000 and 70,000 thoughts enter our mind each day, influencing how we perceive the world and conduct our lives. If we are not consciously monitoring the thoughts that float into our minds from different sources every minute of the day, we can become robots to the whims and desires of others.

Our society bombards us with thoughts and ideas through music, television, podcasts, Internet, phones, and the list goes on. If we are not thinking about what is being said or conveyed, we can allow negative seeds (thoughts) to be deposited into our fertile soil

7 Goodreads.com

(subconscious mind), and we'll be regurgitating someone else's thoughts or behavior.

There was a song I really liked, and I'd sing along whenever I heard it. One day after I'd started being more aware of my environment, I was intentionally listening to the words of this song, and to my surprise, I realized that "Me and Mrs. Jones" were having an illicit affair. Not that having an extramarital affair was on my "list of things to do," but my subconscious mind was receiving it as a good thing.

I think about some of the music out today where women are called b...., and women themselves call each other that now. Young girls thinking it is okay to have a pimp on a bike, and to exploit their bodies like the women on the videos. This is all the result of thoughts and messages not being consciously monitored.

There is a new buzzword going around these days called "mindfulness," which means "the quality or state of being conscious or aware of something." When we stay mindful of the thoughts and ideas we entertain, we can filter out the ones that will not benefit us and nurture the ones that will. Staying aware all the time allows us to monitor what is going on around us and how it is affecting our behavior.

When I started being more aware of the thoughts and messages I was receiving, I began learning more about myself. I noticed that I would get irritated about things not really knowing why. I realized that when I was being irritated by the way someone talked, laughed, or anything that I needed to check myself. I'm not sure where this pattern of behavior originated, but being mindful helped me to change it. Monitoring our thoughts helps us to rewire our brains to aid us in bringing into our lives the things we want and the behavior we want to exhibit.

AFFIRMATIONS

One of the methods that can assist in changing our pattern of thinking is affirmations. An affirmation is defined as "the action or process of affirming something or being affirmed." Affirmations can be an emotional support or encouragement, and the beauty is that the support can come from ourselves. The key is to affirm our goals or achievement with emotion, like we've already achieved it and it's the way we feel. As stated before, our subconscious is subjective so if we are planting excitement with the affirmation, it receives the thought or message as accomplished, and its next job is to bring it to reality.

The first affirmation I used was, "I love and accept myself unconditionally." I chose that particular one because as I stated before, I grew up in an environment tainted with a lot of criticism and a lack of demonstrated love or encouragement. The irony is that I had started feeling better about myself and then I remarried at 21 to my second husband. I was married to him for 12 years and had seven children from this union. This turned out to be a physically abusive relationship. The abuse spiraled me back to a state of not feeling worthy, loved or good enough. I attempted a few times to leave the relationship, but he would always talk me back into staying. I was finally able to leave the abuse through the help of a domestic violence shelter a friend told me about.

I still say this affirmation whenever I experience any doubts about my abilities or position in life to remind me that loving myself is the first order of business after G-D. When I love myself, I can give love to the rest of the world.

VISUALIZATION

Another tool that helps to influence our subconscious mind is visualization, which means to " formulate a mental image of something." With this tool, we can visualize ourselves having anything we'd like to see in our life—whether it's something concrete, abstract or a behavior. In the book *Think and Grow Rich*, by Napoleon Hill, he says:

> *"Whatever the mind can conceive and believe, the mind can achieve"*

Take note of the key word in that statement, *believe.* We need to truly believe with feeling that what we see is doable and that we deserve to have it. That belief becomes the fertilizer that nurtures the seed (our vision) planted in the subconscious mind. In my experience, being able to see that which you are striving for accelerates the process.

To assist in my visualization, I created a vision board in 2012 with pictures and words from magazines of the things that I wanted and was striving for. For example, I wanted to remarry after my 4th divorce so I put a picture of some wedding rings with the words *soul mate* next to them; a picture of a Jaguar which was my dream car; pictures of different countries and the words about traveling; and pictures of confident looking people.

The results of this vision board? I remarried in 2016 to my soulmate; I purchased my Jaguar in 2014; I traveled to Senegal in 2017, and to Italy in 2018; and my level of confidence has soared since 2012. Alhamdulilah!!! (All praises due to G-D)!

Now, one other thing that needs to be included with your visualization is action. You must be doing something daily towards your goal along with your affirmations and visualization. If getting married is one of your goals, create an affirmation such as, "Marriage is my goal, and I am ready for it." Then repeat that affirmation daily with feeling. You could also put it on a mirror or a wall, so you see it often, and also let people know. If it's to travel, start looking at travel brochures or putting up pictures of the places you'd like to go.

Finally, have faith. Faith keeps us moving forward, knowing that our humble servant will get us there if we do our part. In the Holy Quran, 3:40-41 G-D says:

40. That the fruit of his striving will soon come in sight;
41. Then will he be rewarded with a reward complete

ACCEPTANCE

When I first started on this journey, it was hard for me to accept that I was worthy of any of the good things of life. Coming from an environment that didn't instill these qualities in me, it took some mindfulness to change my paradigm. Once I started really loving myself, my decisions were more in line with what was best for me and all concerned.

As stated before, a dear friend who has returned to G-D, told me 30 plus years ago that I would be a writer. At that time, I couldn't see myself even writing the essay she was reviewing for my college application. I had very little confidence, and becoming a writer wasn't something I could see myself doing. But here I am typing away and feeling very confident in the process.

Once we start planting positive seeds about ourselves and accepting that " G-D Don't Make

No Junk," we will realize that we can do and be whatever we want. So many people are dissatisfied with themselves that the plastic surgeons are having a field day; the cosmetic world is making a killing, and people are ending their lives because they are unhappy with who they are. We must believe in ourselves and accept ourselves unconditionally.

We all have a purpose. It's our job to seek it out if we're not sure, so we can unearth our treasures and become the best that we can be.

Your Incredible Mind Action

For the next three days, be very intentional in monitoring what you say to yourself throughout the day and capture it here. Evaluate whether each thought is in your best interest. If not, reject it.

It's not what we say out loud that really determines our lives. It's what we whisper to ourselves that has the most power.

Day 1

Day 2

Day 3

CHAPTER 3
Family

"We are all born with a clean slate, it's our environment that shapes us into the person we become".

- Paraphased from a Hadith (a saying of Prophet Muhammad-PBUH)

CULTURAL INFLUENCE

THE SAYING, "THE apple doesn't fall far from the tree" is a saying I have found to be true. Our family and environment can have a great influence on how we move in this life; however, the blessing is that we have the ability to change those areas that do not benefit us.

I grew up in a household that believed that Caucasians were better and that African

Americans weren't about much. As I mentioned previously, my mother's parenting was void of promoting worthiness or making one feel valued, which was the message she received. She repeated what she knew.

Her claim to fame was being independent, not having to depend on anyone, and being able to dress nice because that wasn't an option for her as a child. She had to wear flour sacks for dresses. For a long time, she distanced herself from her family because of her negative childhood experience.

Aside from my influences at home, my thinking was also shaped by the sitcoms that were popular in the '50s and '60s, which depicted Caucasians as intelligent, successful, and family-oriented. Shows like *Ozzie and Harriet, Leave It To Beaver*, and *Father Knows Best*.

Up until the 70's, the only portrayal of African Americans on television was a program called *Amos & Andy*, which portrayed African Americans as deceitful, ignorant, lazy, and lacking good family values.

The message that was prevalent in these shows reinforced my mother's mindset, which gave value to the Caucasians and worthlessness to the African Americans. These popular sitcoms were humorous, but the contrast in lifestyles were strikingly different. Even the sitcoms that began to air in the 70's didn't portray a positive depiction of African Americans.

In the environments in which I lived, some of the people would imitate the buffoonery of the African American characters in these sitcoms and take it on as an identity for themselves. The overall spirit of a lot of the people I was influenced by was tainted with low self-esteem, self-hatred, and no sense of value.

Values

The word *value* means "standards or ideals with which we evaluate actions, people, things, or situations considered important in life." This was not the standard which those in my environment lived by. Most of the behaviors I saw came out of feelings of self-hate, unworthiness, and hopelessness. I realized later that this mentality was the residual of slavery.

My sense of value was very low as I matured into a young adult. I hadn't been taught that a woman's body was sacred and that I should be married before cohabiting with a man. Most of the people in my environment had what they called common-law marriages, which meant that couples would just start living together without the sanctity of marriage.

I credit this attitude and other behaviors for my becoming pregnant at age 16. Although sex before marriage was an excepted norm, teen pregnancy was frowned upon. Being pregnant was another blow to my self-esteem and feeling of worthiness because I was viewed as a "fast and bad girl." The father of the child wanted to get married, but coming from my frame of reference, I didn't see the point. However, with his persistence, we were married. The marriage only lasted a short time, because he became incarcerated before our daughter was born, and being young I moved on with my life.

WORTHINESS

I thank G-D for the Nation of Islam (NOI), which was an exclusively African American ideology that was designed to uplift the people of African descent. This was the beginning of my moving from feeling insignificant to valuing my worth. The ideology wasn't totally based on truth, but it gave the descendants of slaves a glimmer of hope and worthiness.

I joined the NOI when I was 18. The message of the movement was that the black man was G-D, and the white man was the devil. Embracing this ideology wasn't hard considering our history. You can imagine if that's the message you're giving to your subconscious mind, you can't help beginning to have a sense of value and worthiness.

To add to my boost of self-esteem, the song "I'm Black & I'm Proud" was popular at that time, which watered and nourished the seeds that were being planted in my subconscious mind. Also, African American women began to embrace their natural curly hair and show pride in it. Prior to this period, most African American women were straightening their hair to remove their natural curl. To wear your hair in its natural state before the late 60's was an embarrassment to most African Americans do to the negative connotation that had been associated with our hair... that it was nappy, coarse, and unmanageable.

This really speaks to how important our environment is in shaping who we are. To hear a parent or anyone in my environment growing up say "nappy headed so & so" or be told "how bad your hair was" was common. So all these positive messages I was receiving transformed how I viewed myself as well as the world around me.

That's why I encourage my children and grandchildren to work hard to instill worthiness in their children—acknowledging their feelings and letting them know they matter and applauding their accomplishments, no matter how insignificant they may seem. We should also give those same acknowledgements and affirmations to ourselves, remembering our worthiness. Again, we must remind ourselves often that " G-D Didn't Make No Junk."

SUPPORT

What I learned during my transformation to a new way of thinking is that you can lose some of your support systems. People who supported you when you were participating in behaviors that weren't good for you, now feel you've deserted them. This was especially true for me when I joined the Nation of Islam. The community was very close-knit and did many things together. Their doctrine and lifestyle were totally different from the life I had been living, and my friends and family thought I had become a part of a cult, and they weren't supporting my new way of thinking.

I've realized through this journey how important it is for us to keep our minds open to new information and consciously evaluate it to determine whether it is something we should accept or reject. The NOI helped me to develop better standards of living, to love my African heritage, and have hope for my future. Through the camaraderie, I began to feel loved and needed. The thoughts and messages I was receiving made me a more progressive thinker and gave me confidence in my abilities as an African American. I started to think of doing things I never thought of doing such as becoming a business owner.

During this time, I became involved with network marketing which was also called multi-level marketing. It is a marketing strategy to sell products or services on commission. The main objective is to recruit people to work under you selling a product or service; the amount that you and your team sells, determines your income. Well, this was where the rubber really hit the road for me on my level of confidence.

The training that was provided was geared toward building your confidence and courage so you could recruit people into the business. This was when I was introduced to a lot of motivational speakers who were recommended for us to read or listen to on a cassette. The common thread that ran through all the speakers was the importance of believing in yourself and changing your mode of thinking.

Your Incredible Mind
Action

Reflect on your relationship with your family and how it has influenced your behavior and the way you move through the world.

CHAPTER 4
Meditation

Meditation is a precise technique for resting the mind and attaining a state of consciousness that is totally different from the normal waking state.

—*Swami Rama*

STILLNESS

WE LIVE IN a world that is filled with noise and movement from the moment we rise in the morning until we lay down at night. Some people immediately turn on the television or some other device when they rise in the morning, allowing the thoughts and messages from different sources into their minds which can be positive or negative.

It is no wonder that stress is a major issue in our country. We are dealing with our own personal problems, mixed with what is happening in our neighborhoods and the rest of the world. Stress and emotional overload can affect our health in various ways such as headaches, body pain, restless nights, and indigestion, just to name a few.

Stillness is what allows our body and mind to rest and take a break. It helps us to get in touch with ourselves and those things around us. When we are constantly in motion, we are not always aware of how our body is feeling, what we're thinking, or what is going on in our environment. Stopping for a minute to take "a chill pill" can have a profound effect on us mentally, physically, and spiritually.

We are so wired to be mentally connected to some man-made device that to sit still seems like a waste of time. When I first started practicing stillness, it was hard to sit for five minutes. I'd be thinking of all the things I needed to do, and being still just felt weird. However, as I continued to practice stillness, I started being more relaxed and aware of how my body felt, and I became more in tune with what I call my Divine connection.

CONNECTION

In Islam, we believe that G-D is the Supreme Being and has control over all things, and as human beings we have a direct connection with our Higher Power. Prophet Muhammad PBUH who was the last of the prophets and who came as an example for all humanity. Before his prophethood, he would remove himself from the hustle and bustle of his environment and retreat to a cave, to seek solitude and ponder over the plight of his people. After many visits to this sanctuary he was sanctioned to be the last Prophet of G-D. The message he received was the antidote for the ills of his people as well as the people of the world.

That was definitely a Divine connection and there will be no more prophets after him, however I believe that when we take the time to be still, we can discover our purpose and tap into our greatness.

In the Holy Quran, 2:186, G-D says:

"When my servants ask you concerning Me-Indeed I am near, I respond to every invocation of the supplicant when he calls upon me. So let them respond to Me that they may be guided."

In Islam we believe that all things in creation are connected and were created by the same source, so it makes sense to me that we can commune with G-D through our time of prayer or our moments of silence and stillness. I believe we can receive revelations during our moments of prayer, meditation, or moments of stillness. I use to associate the word *revelation* with scriptures, but when I looked it up, I found that the word means "a surprising and previously unknown fact, especially one that is made known in a dramatic way."

It is so exciting to me to know that we are all connected to the Power Source of all creation and that we can shine like the sun and be a source of light for others, using the gift of our mind.

Intuition

The term *intuition* is defined as, "The ability to understand something immediately, without the need for conscious reasoning." For example, we might think of a person, and they will call or come by. Recently my ex-husband had been on my mind, and I was wondering whether he was okay. My intention was to check with his daughter, but I didn't. Then a few days later,

I heard he'd collapsed and had to go to the hospital. This understanding [intuition] comes in my opinion from our Divine source.

Everytime this type of incident happens I remember my mother saying "always follow your first mind." How many times have you said, "I should have followed my first mind"? What mind is that? As far as I know, we as humans only have one, but I believe that other mind comes from our Divine source. That's why in Al-Islam whenever we remember something or things happen that was out of our control, we say: "Alhamdulilah" (All praised to G-D) because HE is the source of everything.

The part of the definition above that says "without the need for conscious reasoning" made me think of our five senses. All stimuli comes in through one of our five senses which is a conscious action. however our intuitive thought comes in without conscious reasoning. In the book the Clear Path to Human Development by Faheem Shuaibe, he states,

> *The five senses connect the inner life of the human being (subjective) to the external world (objective). They conduct the essence of the environment into the interior and transform them into inputs that enable the brain to experience and understand the information and derive meaning from those sources. (Pg 34)*

Alhamdulilah, that statement for me just reaffirms my belief that our intuition is from our Divine source. It's independent of our conscious mind. When we began the process of self growth and development, listening and responding to our intuitive thoughts are important. It's another gift from G-D to help us advance to the next level of our growth and development.

Focus

To focus means to center our attention on an interest or activity. In *The Power of Focus*, there's a quote from Charles Dickens, which says, "I never could have done without the habits of punctuality, order and diligence and the determination to concentrate myself on one subject at a time."[8] We live in a time when multitasking is the thing to do. Most of us are doing different tasks at the same time not giving our full attention to any one thing. We often switch between tasks without taking a break. This has not proven to be good for our productivity on our job and in our personal life.

A research study on multitasking featured in the October 8, 2014 edition of *Forbes* from the forbes.com archives, found that "multitasking reduces your efficiency and performance because the brain can only focus on one thing at a time effectively. In addition it can slow you down, and can lower your IQ." This article also stated "that people who are regularly bombarded with several streams of electronic information do not pay attention, recall information, or switch from one job to another as well as those who complete one task at a time."

To make the changes we want in life, we need to gain control over how we move through our day. This requires that we plan our days so that what we are striving to incorporate into our life is included into our daily routine. We

8   Jack Canfield, Mark V. Hansen, and Les Hewitt, *The Power of Focus* (Deerfield Beach, FL: Health Communications, Inc, 2000), Page 30
9. Forbes.com archives

usually go through our days on automatic pilot not giving much thought to the task at hand. To bring into our life our desires and wants, we have to focus. That requires monitoring our thoughts and how they are helping us to reach our goal. This is when affirmations and meditation can be useful.

For instance, when I had to reincorporate exercise in my life, I initially had to consciously coax my body to get up and get moving. Once I was up and moving, I'd focus on what I was doing and the benefits I was deriving from it. This was reinforcing the message I wanted to plant in my subconscious mind. I've heard that when you focus on what you're doing and why, you get more benefit from the action. Now the thought of exercising has become a part of my daily routine.

In meditation, it is recommended that you say a mantra, which can be a word or phase that you repeat, an object that you focus on, or music or nature sounds. The mantra helps you keep your focus during meditation. When your mind wanders—as it will, the mantra helps you to refocus. What I've gained through meditation is that it helps me stay focused at other times of the day which helps me to stay calm in my spirit, and I seem to get more done.

Letting Go

Meditation is the go-to place to let go of all the hustle and bustle of the world and sink into a space of peace. It can be a humbling experience because you let go of trying to control the situations in your life. What I've learned over the years is that I only have control over myself and how I think or respond to any situation. Once I accepted that G-D has control over everything, even what happens in my life, it allowed me to let go of the outcome and just do what is in my power.

My biggest challenge of "letting go" came in 1985 when my youngest child who was two years old at the time, travelled to Sudan the birthplace of his father, my third husband. The trip was to be for a 3-4 month visit with his family. To my horror, three months turned into 3 years. The communication between his father and I ended after about 6 months and I wasn't sure if that meant I would never see my son again.

As a means of keeping my sanity I started saying the Serenity Prayer which I still say daily:

> *"G-D grant me the serenity to accept the things I cannot change, courage to change the things I can, and the wisdom to know the difference"*

With little money and even less connections, I wasn't in a position to travel to Sudan. But after talking with various people about my circumstance, I was directed to the then Assemblyman George Miller. After a series of contacts with the American Embassy in Sudan, we learned that my son was being cared for by my then husband's relatives and he seemed in good health and spirit. The family informed the embassy that his father was working out of the country,

Shortly thereafter, his father contacted me letting me know that they would be returning. Now you can only imagine the joy I felt upon seeing my son. I was initially still angry with his father, however we eventually tried to reconcile but it didn't work. The lessons I learned through this experience have stayed with me forever.

Your Incredible Mind
Action

Sit for 3 to 5 minutes and concentrate on the word *relax* or any other positive, peaceful word. If you are not into meditation, when your mind starts to wander, simply recognize it and return back to your word. Notice how you feel after your first session. Once you're able to do 5 minutes, start increasing the time until you can do 20 minutes.

CHAPTER 5
Inner Circle

"And keep thy soul content with those who call on their Lord morning and evening, seeking HIS Face' and let not thine eyes pass beyond them seeking the pomp and glitter of this life' nor obey any whose heart We have permitted to neglect the remembrance of Us, one who follows his own desires, whose case has gone beyond all bounds."

The Holy Quran, 18:28

LIKE MINDS

ON THIS JOURNEY through life, we change many things along the way such as our professions, religious preferences, hobbies, educational pursuits, and so on. Change is hard, so having someone who is supporting your decisions makes the transition easier.

In Al Islam and other religions, we are encouraged to seek help from the Supreme Being as support through our endeavors.

"Fear not I am with you, do not be dismayed, for I am your G-D, I will strengthen you. I will help you"

(Isaiah 41:10)

Oh you who have believed seek help through patience and prayer Indeed, G-D is with the patient"

(The Holy Quran, 2:153)

G-D also helps through his servants. For example, when I decided to return to school, I was in my 40s, and my confidence level was still very low. I discussed it with family members and friends, and I got some high fives from some and "Are you sure?" from others. The catalyst that helped me to take the plunge was the strength I gained from my children that supported the decision and rallied me on until I graduated.

I've learned that in whatever endeavor we embark on we need to have people around us who are of a like mind. To stay committed to a new way of thinking or doing something new requires having the right messages being planted in our subconscious mind to reinforce our objective.

Edmund Jennings Lee, a prominent legal and political figure in Alexandria, Virginia, said:

"Surround yourself with the dreamers and the doers, the believers and thinkers, but most of all, surround yourself with those who see the greatness within you, even when you don't see it yourself."

The actress Doris Day said:

"Encourage, lift and strengthen one another: For the positive energy spread to one will be felt by us all. For we are connected, one and all."

In the Holy Bible, Proverbs 13:20 says:

"Whoever walks with the wise becomes wise, but the companion of fools will suffer harm."

As your consciousness becomes deeper and your intuition becomes firmer, you will begin to hear your inner voice, which speaks to you always. This is when your spiritual awakening will take place, and it will spread across your whole being. Keep your inner circle small, sacred, and pure.

- Avijeet Das- (Goodreads.com)

Spiritual Mates

What I've come to realize is that is all our relationships are from a spiritual place, being that we are spiritual beings having a human experience. We all have probably had the experience of meeting someone and it seems like we've known them forever. And for someone else, the energy between you can seem strange, and really don't know why.

On a universal level we are all connected so it makes sense that we would have spiritual encounters. I believe there are different levels of spiritual connections and that a spiritual soul mate is more kindred in spirit than others. My mother used to say, "You will have a lot of associates, but very few real friends." On a spiritual level I know that to be true.

This is especially important when creating your inner circle. It should be those of like mind, who are supportive, will hold you accountable in a loving and caring way, and you enjoy being around them. Accomplishing our goals in this life is challenging, and most of us need that extra push to cross the finish line. This has been my experience with my spiritual comrades, who have believed in my dreams and have provided me with the spiritual wings to ascend toward my greatness.

There's an east asian philosophy that says:

"A soulmate is someone who has locks that fit our keys, and keys to fit our locks. When we feel safe enough to open the locks, our truest selves step out and we can be completely and honestly who we are."

Your Incredible Mind Action

Give some thought to who's in your Amen corner.

1. Who will support your efforts and be your accountability partner?

2. Are you surrounding yourself with people of like mind with whom you have a spiritual connection?

CHAPTER 6
Know Thy Self

STRENGTHS

OUR STRENGTHS ARE those things that come easy for us—things we're good at and like. A strength can also be a skill that we've learned and do very well. Identifying our strengths is not something most of us think about until we are asked.

For a long time, I wasn't sure what my strengths and weaknesses were. Part of my problem was that I was looking at weaknesses as a negative, which they are not. But I was not alone; I've found that a lot of people don't know how to identify their strengths and weaknesses. This is a question we ask when interviewing potential employees and the response is usually, "You know, I haven't thought about that." Although some applicants can answer very quickly what their weaknesses are, most haven't embraced what they do well.

I discovered that knowing your strengths can help you make better choices in your careers and other facets of your life. When we can acknowledge our strengths and what we do well, it will boost how we feel about ourselves. If you're not sure what your strengths are, take some time to really think about what you like to do and what comes easy for you. Ask those close to you what they think your strengths are because oftentimes, others see us better than we see ourselves.

I compared myself to others for many years. I'm basically an introvert with extrovert qualities. That is, I can spend a lot of time by myself and be very content. I also like to engage with people and do various activities but, at times, that can be overwhelming. In the past, when I was around people who were very outgoing, I would feel inferior because I thought I should be like them. Even though we may instinctively know that everyone is different, we can easily forget that in the moment. When I finally embraced my introverted nature, I no longer viewed it as a negative. .

It's important to understand that our weaknesses are not a negative thing; it's simply areas that we need to work on. One of the areas I had to work on was initiating conversation with strangers. I felt a little awkward when I first started initiating conversations, but now I feel very comfortable. I've met some very interesting people that I may not have met if I hadn't strengthened that area of my life.

Life is very interesting. In the end, some of your greatest pains become your greatest strengths.

—Drew Barrymore, actress, producer, director, author, model, and entrepreneur

CHALLENGES

Ironically, challenges are our friends. G-D places them before us so we can discover our strengths and abilities. Our growth and development are a result of the challenges and difficulties we have encountered.

Our very beginning was a challenge. Getting through the birth canal for some of us was no small feat, but that was our entry into this world, and then we were bombarded with bright lights and strange faces. Then, we had to work at getting the milk to flow so we could be nourished; and cry to get our needs met. We fell many times trying to learn how to walk and sustained many injuries getting to know our world. But through it all, we survived and evolved into the person we are today.

In the Holy Quran, 96:5-8, G-D (swt) says:

---

5. So, verily, with every difficulty there is relief;
6. Verily with every difficulty there is relief;
7. Therefore, when thou art free (from thine immediate task), still labour hard;
8. And to thy Lord turn thy attention

A saying one of my daughters would always say was, "If it doesn't kill you, it will just make you stronger." I've found this to be true on this journey. I have encountered many challenges, especially raising my children, and each time, I couldn't see the light at the end of the tunnel. Then the light would come shining through, and sometimes I'd understand why the challenge was necessary, and other times I didn't, but I'd always be a much wiser and stronger person in the end.

Attitude plays a big part in how we deal with challenges. I've learned that the first thing I need to do when confronted with a challenge is to accept that it's not going away, that I can't run from it, and that G-D never gives me something I can't handle. I will then put the issue in perspective, which oftentimes isn't as overwhelming as I first thought, seek help if needed, and then pray.

Our first African American First Lady of the United States, Michelle Obama said:

"You should never view your challenges as a disadvantage. Instead, it's important for you to understand that your experience of facing and overcoming adversity is actually one of your biggest advantages."

BEHAVIORS

Previously I mentioned the importance of having a good attitude when dealing with challenges, but it is also important in monitoring our behavior in any given situation.. Our behaviors can be an asset or a liability. The good news is that a lot of our behaviors are learned, which means they can be changed.

My mother did not like for me to ask questions, and she would usually get upset when I did. She was conditioned in an environment where children should be seen and not heard. That proved to be stifling and counterproductive for me because as an adult when I should have been asking questions, I didn't.

When I started monitoring my thoughts and actions, I noticed one day that I said to one of my children, "Don't ask so many questions." A feeling of shame came over me and I asked myself, "What did you just say, and why shouldn't they ask questions?" In that moment, I realized the negative repercussion that behavior had on my growth and development, and decided right then to not pass on that behavior.

I started monitoring my behavior and what I said to my children, and in other areas of my life to ensure that I wasn't presenting myself in a negative way. Being more self aware helped me to see myself in a different light, and to start creating the person I wanted to be.

This was not an overnight process; it took some time to change the behaviors because they had become habits. The good news is that when you start being aware of your thoughts and actions, you can respond or react to any situation appropriately. It was Plato who said, *"Human behavior flows from three main sources; desire, emotion, and knowledge."*

ACCOMPLISHMENTS

It is important to stop and think about our journey as humans and acknowledge who we have become and what we have achieved. For a long time, women weren't acknowledged for their contribution to humanity, and we would even downplay our contributions to our families, friends, community, and the world. Unfortunately, this attitude still exists today in this country and other areas of the world.

In this country, when women started to acknowledge their worth and value and the accomplishments they were making to their communities and the world, their lives changed and became more productive. It is important that we take the time to evaluate and reflect on the things we have done and acknowledge and claim our accomplishments. This knowledge can change how we feel about ourselves and can inspire us to do other things that we may have thought we couldn't do.

I have nine wonderful children, 7 girls and 2 boys, who I mostly raised alone. For a long time, I focused on what I hadn't done as a parent instead of what I had.. It wasn't until my children became adults and were having children of their own, that I started to hear from them what a good job they felt I had done. Of course, I made many mistakes along the way, but as I say now, "If I had known better, I would have done better." I now acknowledge the accomplishments I've made, and which has been another boost in my feeling of self-worth and value.

We all like to be acknowledged, but the greatest acknowledgment is what we give ourselves. Henry Wadsworth Longfellow, an American poet, said: *"Man is always more than he can know of himself, consequently, his accomplishments, time and again, will come as a surprise to him"*

So celebrate your accomplishments, and feel good about who you are, cause we all are special and unique.

LOVE THY SELF

It's amazing how many people in the world do not love themselves unconditionally. With all the plastic surgery and self-destructive behaviors we see today, it is a testimony that self-love is not the order of the day. The sad part is it is affecting our society at a much younger age.

The images that are portrayed as the standard of beauty have distorted our sense of self, especially I feel, in the African American community. I remember as a young girl I didn't want to take swimming lessons because my hair would return to its naturally curly state, which I stated before was not a good look to African Americans. Many of us wanted straight hair like the Caucasain women It wasn't until the 60's and 70's that nappy hair became a sign of pride, and our community started loving that side of ourselves that was despised.

We have to love ourselves unconditionally in order to grow and develop into our full potential. As was stated earlier G-D made us in the best of moulds and to be our true and authentic selves we have to embrace our whole self.

It saddens me that some of us are still trying to fit in, by altering our true identity when it comes to our hair. I've realized in my own experience that when I acknowledge and show pride in who I am, it feels good. The most beautiful people I've encountered over the years were those who would be considered ugly by the American standard, but who exhibited a demeanor that was full of life and pride in who they were. When we truly love ourselves unconditionally our greatness and beauty radiates out to the world.

Remember that you are always with yourself, so you might as well enjoy the company.

Your Incredible Mind Action

Reflect and then write down:

1. Your strengths

2. Accomplishments (no matter how seemingly small)

3. What you love about yourself

4. Your greatest challenge thus far

5. Behavior(s) you'd like to change (if any)

An Invitation

*I*T CAN SEEM unbelievable and sometimes overwhelming when we first really embrace the fact that we can literally change our course in life by just changing the way we think. Realizing that we all have something unique within us that we can share with the world or at least our community, by just becoming the navigator of our destiny is beyond beautiful. Are you ready to take the plunge to reprogram your subconscious mind?

My *Incredible Mind 90 Day Program* can be the answer. The program is designed to give you the tools needed to erase the old tapes, help you discover or start moving toward your purpose, and replant new ideas and thoughts in your subconscious mind. It is the support you need to reach your desired destiny.

Just think about it, the first humans on earth had nothing but the plants, trees, animals, fish — humble beginnings. Human beings had to learn to create fire to warm themselves, to cook their food, to fly like a bird, to travel on and under the ocean and sea, and to talk with each other through wires and now with no wires. All these accomplishments came from people's minds — the same mind we all possess.

It has been said that we only use 10 percent of our mind capacity. I believe that at the inception of the human being on this earth, we probably were using 100 percent of our mind capacity, but over time, we started using less of this incredible power. Think about the pyramids and how the minds of today are still trying to figure out how that feat was accomplished. To accomplish these and other ancient feats, they must have used more than 10 percent of their brain capacity and to me the pyramids are a testament to that reality. We were created with the ability to transform any environment we are put into and to do amazing things.

I pray you complete the exercises presented in the book and that you began to see results. By becoming the captain of your own ship, you can leave a legacy for the generations to come and provide a brighter future for you and your family. If you planted a seed at some point in your journey that you wanted to do but thought you couldn't at the time, or a new endeavor you'd like to try, I'd encourage you to revisit it. If G-D has presented you with some seeds of possibilities, HE knows you can do it. There are so many things that have not yet come into existence —things that may be lying dormant in your fertile soil waiting to be discovered and nurtured.

This world is our oyster, and we must work to get out our pearls. Our brain with its mystic component called the subconscious mind is at our beck and call. We just need to trust and use it. My prayer is that I've given you some inspiration to learn more about your incredible mind that will work together to give you your heart's desire. This book has been a long time coming, but *Your Incredible Mind* is now here. Once I started watering the seed (thoughts) of writing a book with belief and faith, the words for each chapter started to blossom from the fertile soil of my subconscious mind.

I truly encourage you to allow your greatness to shine through and share with the world your own precious gems.

Lastly, I'd love to read your review of the book on Amazon and hear from you. Also if you'd like to contact me for questions or more information about my program please email me at beaboutyourmind@gmail.com.

May G-D be with you.

About the Author

Zarinah El-Amin Majied is a certified health and mindset coach from California who helps people at a crossroads to orchestrate their desired destiny and live their best life.

In 1993, she co-founded with two of her daughters, MU'EED Inc, a non-profit corporation, which operates social programs including Our Children's Keeper Child & Family Services, a foster care agency. This work provides a window into the struggles of many of the parents who haven't been taught how to affect the change they wish to see in their lives.

Zarinah wants to make access to this type of knowledge far spreading.

She is the proud and blessed mother of 9 children, 28 grandchildren and 15 great-grand-children. After four marriages and many struggles, Zarinah is now happily and peace-fully married and is continuing to do the work necessary to live her best life.

To learn more about how you can work with Zarinah privately and get support, please email her at BeAboutYourMind@gmail.com.

www.BeAboutYourMind.com

Made in the USA
Monee, IL
19 July 2021